D1221112

Sept. 17th, '88

A Day in the Life of Diana

Princess of Wales

To Linda,

Love,
Carol

A Day in the Life of Diana

Princess of Wales

Brenda R. Lewis

Studio Publications, Ipswich

A Day in the Life of Diana

Princess of Wales

WHAT does a princess do all day? In fairy tales, princesses sew or listen to minstrels singing, or take walks in the garden. They don't seem to do very much, really.

Life is very different for a real-life princess like Diana, Princess of Wales. If you could see Diana's diary, you would find it full of all sorts of activities. She visits hospitals, factories and shipyards. She goes to schools and community centres. Everywhere, people gather in big crowds, hoping to get the chance to look at her. The lucky ones shake Diana's hand and talk with her. Diana always tries to talk to as many people as she can, because she knows they are there, especially to see her.

Diana also goes to film performances and concerts in aid of charity. She is very interested in children. Before she married Charles, Prince of Wales, in 1981, she worked as a teacher in a kindergarten school. Today, she does a lot of work to help organisations which care for children. Because she is a member of the Royal Family, Diana also attends big royal events, like the State Opening of Parliament. Sometimes, with Prince Charles, she goes on long journeys to far-away places like Australia and Canada.

Of course, Diana can sometimes spend a quiet day at home with her two sons. But as you can see, her life is a very busy one. She has to be away from her children quite a lot.

Right: *Lady Diana Spencer, before her marriage, with two of the children she cared for in the New England Kindergarten.*

Below: *Fairy Tale Princess marries her Prince Charming.*

The Princess of Wales receives hundreds of invitations from many different people. There are too many for her to accept all of them. But once she has said "Yes", there is a lot of work to do. A timetable has to be worked out for her visit. The Princess has to study information about the place she is going to visit and what she will see. Arrangements are made for her to travel there. The detectives who look after Diana's security, must make sure she will be safe during her visit.

Before the Princess leaves home for a public engagement or visit, she spends time with her children, Prince William and Prince Harry and talks with their nanny, Barbara Barnes. The Princess must dress carefully for the engagement in suitable clothes. With the help of her maid, she does her hair so that it will look attractive all day.

Why does Diana have public engagements?
The Princess of Wales, like other members of the Royal Family, undertakes a lot of public engagements. This means she makes visits to places to see how people live and work, or how they are cared for when they are ill. Why does the Princess do all this? The reason is that the Royal Family think it important to show they are interested in ordinary people. They want to know about people's problems and if they can help them. The Royal Family believe it is their duty to do these things and in return, the people admire and respect the Royal Family.

Opposite: *Charles and Diana were very glad to be reunited on the Royal Yacht Britannia with their two sons, Prince William and Prince Henry on their Italian tour.*

Diana goes to Scotland Yard

Today, the Princess of Wales is visiting Scotland Yard. This is the headquarters of the Metropolitan Police in London. The Princess arrives at a quarter past ten in the morning. She herself asked if she could see the work of the police force in Scotland Yard, so she is very excited about it.

The Princess is wearing a dark red outfit with a white collar and red tie, but no hat. When she comes into the building, a woman police officer presents her with a beautiful bunch of

Right: *The Princess of Wales was very excited to visit Scotland Yard. Here she is meeting Sir Kenneth Newman, the Commissioner of Police.*

The People Who Help Diana

The Princess of Wales needs many people to help her so that her public engagements will run smoothly. She has to have people to run her homes for her and help her look after her children. Diana is a very devoted mother and she likes to care for her children herself when she can. Both she and Prince Charles give them their baths. And when Prince William was getting his first teeth, the Princess stayed up with him for many hours during the night. 'Teething' is painful, so William was lucky to have his mother to comfort him.

All the same, the Princess is very busy, so she needs a nanny who can look after her sons when she is away. She also has a cook-housekeeper to make meals and other staff to do the housework.

Right: *Barbara Barnes is the young nanny Diana chose for her children.*

flowers. The Princess carries these flowers with her as she is taken on a tour of the building.

The first thing the Princess sees is the Traffic Control Section. Here, there are lots of television screens. They show the cars and buses moving along the busy streets of London. The pictures are taken by TV cameras placed at the most crowded crossroads. The Princess is able to watch the traffic moving along and learns how the police control it so that there are no traffic jams: they just alter the timing of

Below: *The Princess enjoys an afternoon at Wimbledon watching the tennis.*

The People Who Help Diana
For her public life as Princess of Wales, Diana has many people to help her with her engagements. She has four ladies-in-waiting. One of them, Anne Beckwith-Smith, works full-time for the Princess. The others work part-time. A lady-in-waiting always goes with the Princess on her public engagements. She walks a little way behind the Princess, ready to help her in any way she can. The lady-in-waiting carries a large handbag. Inside are a sewing kit for emergency repairs, some tissues and a copy of the timetable for the visit. If the Princess is going to make a speech, the lady-in-waiting carries a copy of that, too. Often, ladies-in-waiting become close personal friends. Diana was accompanied by a lady-in-waiting when she visited the Royal Box at the Wimbledon Tennis Championships.

Right: *The Princess of Wales and her Lady-in-Waiting Anne Beckwith-Smith enjoy an informal chat during a public engagement in the Isle of Wight.*

the traffic lights! Next, the Princess sees the National Identification Bureau. Here, she watches policemen and women operating the computers which help them find out about people who commit crimes.

During her visit, which has lasted almost two hours, the Princess has also seen Scotland Yard's own museum and signed her name in the Visitor's Book.

The Princess leaves Scotland Yard at twelve o'clock. The first engagement of the day is over, but there are more to come. It is going to be a busy day.

The People Who Help Diana

Another person who always accompanies the Princess of Wales when she goes out is her personal detective or bodyguard. His job is to make sure the Princess is safe, so he keeps a close watch on the crowds and the streets round about to make sure everything is all right.

The Princess has two chief helpers who organise her public engagements. One is her Private Secretary who deals with letters and telephone calls for the Princess. The Secretary also finds out information about the places the Princess is going to visit and deals with arrangements for those visits.

Then there is the Princess's Equerry. He is the man who organises the Princess's timetable. He arranges the time at which she arrives at engagements and the time she leaves. If the Princess has to change her clothes between engagements, the Equerry must make sure she has enough time to do this. He must also make sure that she can have a short rest between one engagement and the next.

Opposite: *The Princess with her bodyguard who helps to keep her safe.*

Above: *Diana enjoys a shopping spree in London.*

The Princess of Wales is a beautiful young woman with a lovely slim figure. Girls like to copy the clothes she wears, so she chooses her clothes very carefully. When new clothes are made for her, she may choose the design from pictures or drawings. She picks the colours from swatches, or bundles, of small pieces of different materials. Sometimes, she sees a dress in a designer's showroom and asks that the same dress be made for her.

The Princess wears bright colours so that she can be seen in large crowds. Her hats must not hide her face, because everyone wants to see her. Sometimes she wears clothes specially to please the people she meets. When the Princess and her husband visited Italy, for instance, she wore a dress in red, white and green. These are the colours of Italy's national flag.

Most of the shoes Diana wears have very low heels. This is because the Princess is very tall. If she wore high heels, she would look a lot taller than her husband. She is 1.7 metres tall. He is 1.8 metres tall, so there is not a lot of difference between them.

Diana has a very lovely skin, so she does not need a lot of make-up. She uses a little rouge on her cheeks and shiny transparent (see-through) lipstick on her lips. Because she is very fair, she makes up her eyes so that they look large. She uses lots of mascara on her eyelashes.

Opposite: *The Princess, in a stylish blue and white spotted suit, presented the end of Summer Term prizes at The Royal Academy of Music; she is the President of the Academy.*

Above: *Diana wears a stunning red outfit with matching tights during her visit to Florence.*

Above: *The Princess grew her hair longer to enable her to wear it in many different styles.*

During the year, members of the Royal Family gather for *State Occasions.* These are important events in which the Queen plays the chief part as Head of State — that is, leader of the country. The Prince of Wales is heir (successor) to the Queen, so he is also in attendance with the Princess of Wales.

State Occasions are full of colour and pageantry. One is Trooping the Colour which takes place in June, on the Queen's official birthday. At this ceremony, a regiment of the British Army 'troops', or carries, its standard (flag) in front of the Queen. The Princess of Wales, with other ladies of the Royal

***Above:** The Royal Family always gather on the Buckingham Palace balcony to greet the crowds after the Trooping the Colour ceremony.*

Family, watches the Trooping and later comes out on to the balcony at Buckingham Palace to greet the crowds outside.

In early November, Queen Elizabeth rides in her State Coach to Westminster to open the new session (meeting) of the Houses of Parliament. The Princess of Wales rode with the Queen in her carriage on one occasion. Like other royal ladies, the Princess wore a long gown and a tiara to show the importance of the event.

In the middle of November, there is a sad ceremony for the Royal Family to attend. This is the Remembrance Day Parade where men killed in the two World Wars and in the Falklands War of 1982 are honoured. The Princess of Wales, dressed in black, watches the ceremony with other members of the Royal Family from a nearby balcony.

Above: *The Queen and the Princess ride to the State Opening of Parliament in the magnificent Irish State Coach.*

Above: *The Royals look sad as they honour Britain's war dead.*

Now that the morning visit is over, it is time to have lunch. The Princess of Wales may feel rather hungry by this time, because usually, she has only a very light breakfast. She is always very careful about what she eats, because she wants to keep herself nice and slim. This is why the Princess exercises every day and does as much swimming as she can. Swimming is very good for the figure and sometimes, the Princess will do thirty lengths of the pool during one weekend. This is not difficult for her, because she loves swimming and was a champion swimmer when she was at school.

At mealtimes, the Princess always chooses foods which are

***Right:** The Prince and Princess of Wales with servicemen at the Falklands War Memorial in London.*

not too fattening. She needs to be very strong-willed to do this because she goes to many important dinners and receptions where the food is very rich. She is fond of shepherd's pie and mushy peas and also likes wine gums, but she tries not to eat *any* of them.

When Diana has a cup of tea, she drinks it without milk or sugar. At lunch time, she prefers a salad to a big meal. Once, when she was in Canada, she was offered a large steak at a barbecue. Instead, she preferred some fresh salmon.

"I have to watch my waistline," she often says. As you can see from her pictures, she does take great care and makes sure she doesn't put on a lot of weight.

Left: *This favourite dress of the Princess of Wales shows off Diana's enviable, slim figure.*

A Visit to the Ideal Home Exhibition

Quite often, when the Princess of Wales comes to a place, lots of children are waiting for her. As you know, she loves children and they love her. In 1985, when the Princess visited the 'Daily Mail' Ideal Home Exhibition at Olympia, a crowd of children rushed towards her carrying small bunches of flowers. Smiling at the children, she took all the flowers before going into the great Exhibition Hall.

The Princess arrived at three in the afternoon. She was wearing a fashionable suit with a short jacket. First, she met and talked with some of the people who worked on the Exhibition.

Below: *The Princess at the Daily Mail Ideal Home Exhibition.*

Diana's Homes

Highgrove House is the country home of the Prince and Princess of Wales. It stands near the village of Tetbury in Gloucestershire and was built about two hundred years ago. There are nine big bedrooms at Highgrove, as well as six bathrooms and a set of nursery rooms for Prince William and Prince Harry. In the grounds of Highgrove House, the Prince and Princess have stables for the horses. There are many farm buildings and very large, very beautiful gardens. Because it lies deep in the countryside, Charles and Diana can go to Highgrove when they want to have a quiet break from their royal duties. They often spend weekends there. Prince Charles' sister, Princess Anne, lives not far away at Gatcombe Park, so that Charles and Diana have royal relatives near by. Diana likes to go down to Tetbury, which is 2½ kilometres from Highgrove, to do her shopping there.

Above: *Highgrove House near Tetbury — Charles and Diana's country home.*

Right: *The Princess and her husband Prince Charles were delighted to open the Westonbirt School in Tetbury.*

Then, together with her Lady-in-Waiting and two royal officials, the Princess was shown round the Exhibition stands. There was a huge rainbow over 21 metres high, decorating the hall. Round the rainbow, there were five 'show houses'. The Princess explored two houses and then looked at the other stands. She was very interested in the ones where kitchens and other gadgets for the home were being shown.

The Princess talked to several

Diana's Homes

Members of the Royal Family have lived at **Kensington Palace** ever since the year 1689. The palace has many apartments. Princess Margaret, sister of the Queen, has one of them. Prince and Princess Michael of Kent have another. So have the Duke and Duchess of Gloucester and the Duke's mother, Princess Alice.

The apartments at Kensington Palace, owned by the Prince and Princess of Wales, are their home in London. It is very important for them to have a home in Britain's capital city because it means they are close to many places where they carry out their public engagements.

At Kensington Palace, the Prince and Princess have four big reception rooms, including a large dining-room and a drawing-room where they can entertain guests. There is also a large 'master' bedroom, nursery rooms for the children and rooms for their servants and staff.

Although the Palace stands in the centre of London, its surroundings look like countryside because it is right next to the beautiful lawns and trees of Kensington Gardens.

Opposite: *The Prince and Princess of Wales live in a double apartment in Kensington Palace when they are resident in London.*

exhibitors and asked them about their products.

After her tour was over, Diana was given two small crystal bottles as a present. She also received a cake decorated with the names of Prince William and Prince Harry in icing and a beautiful portrait of herself, embroidered in Chinese silk. It took one hundred days to make.

The Princess was supposed to stay for one and a half hours, but she was so interested in the Exhibition that she stayed for thirty minutes more. When she left, at about five o'clock, she probably had many new ideas for her own homes.

Above: *Diana's mother, the Hon. Mrs. Shand Kydd.*

Above: *Diana's father, Lord Spencer.*

Above: *Diana lived at Althorp House when she was a child.*

Diana's Homes

Althorp in Northamptonshire is the family seat or chief home of the Princess of Wales' family. Before her marriage, the Princess was Lady Diana Spencer and her father, who now owns Althorp, is the eighth Earl Spencer.

Althorp is a splendid place, more like a palace than a house. It has an enormous entrance hall and a big wide staircase made of oak. The house is over three hundred years old and stands in beautiful grounds, with vast green lawns. The gardens contain a lake and a Roman-style temple made of wood.

When the Princess was a little girl, she spent a lot of time at another of the Spencer family homes, Park House, near the Queen's home at Sandringham. But, of course, she often came to Althorp and today, members of the public are allowed to visit the house. So, if you like, you can see for yourself the house where Diana once lived.

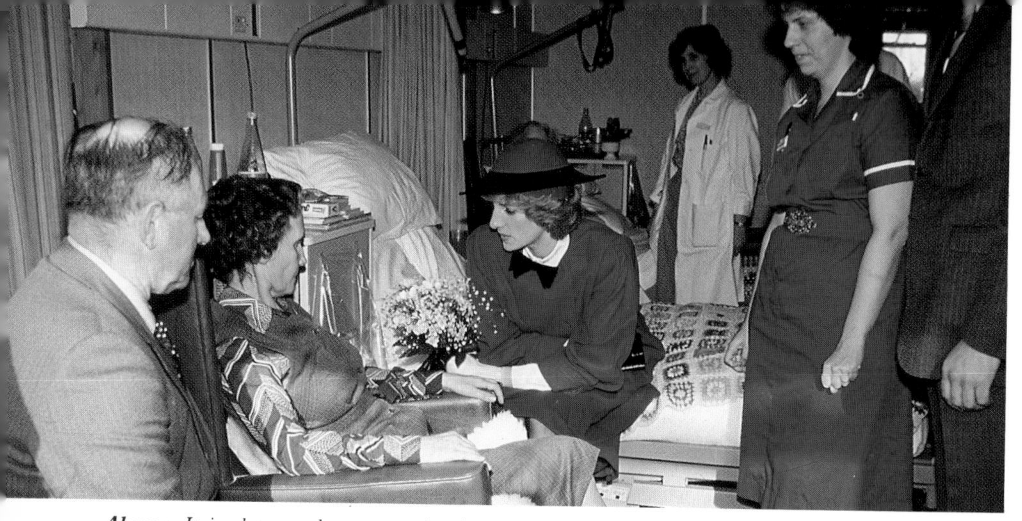

Above: *It is always a happy occasion for patients in hospital when the Princess of Wales comes to cheer them up. Here Diana visits the Clementine Churchill Hospital in Harrow.*

The Princess of Wales has an interesting life. She does something different every day. One day, she may visit a children's hospital or go to a television station and see how TV programmes are broadcast. Another day, she will be at a new shopping centre or a factory. Other days, she sees how a fire brigade works or she visits a regiment of the British Army and learns how soldiers live and work. Another day, she may visit the Royal Navy.

In June 1985, for example, the Princess embarked on (went on to) the Royal Navy frigate 'Beaver' at Portland, in Dorset. 'Beaver' sailed out to sea. For three hours, the Princess watched the crew of the ship at work and saw their complicated equipment in operation.

The Princess also gets a chance to look at Britain's past history.

For instance, in May 1985, she visited Maiden Castle in Dorset: the famous King Arthur fought a big battle near this Iron Age hill fort over 1,500 years ago.

The Princess of Wales also spends some very interesting evenings. In February 1985, she went to 10 Downing Street, London, the home of the Prime Minister, and met young people from countries overseas. Other evenings, there are concerts, films or fashion shows to attend.

On some engagements, the Princess goes with her husband, the Prince of Wales. On other occasions, the Prince and Princess have different engagements. Whether they are apart or together during the day, they have interesting things to talk about when they get home.

Below: *Two "Royal Princesses". Diana launches the P&O Liner "Royal Princess" at Southampton.*

Wales is a sort of 'kingdom' for Prince Charles, the Prince of Wales. It is called a 'Principality', that is the domain of a prince.

After their marriage in 1981, Prince Charles took the Princess to Wales to introduce her to the people. This was her first important public engagement. The Welsh gave their new Princess a marvellous welcome. Everyone wanted to shake her hand. In fact, she shook so many hands that afterwards, her own hand was red and sore!

Since then, Charles and Diana have visited Wales many times. When they are there, they go to Welsh towns like Cardiff or Rhyl. They visit centres for old people or schools and hospitals. And in 1985, they went to the first concert of the famous Eisteddfod at Clwyd.
This is a festival where people come from all over the world to perform music or read poetry.

Above: *A visit to Clwyd, Wales.*

Why 'Princess of Wales'?

Why is Prince Charles the Prince of Wales?

The reason goes back to the year 1284 when Edward I was King of England. For many years, King Edward had fought against the princes in Wales. By 1284, the last of them had been defeated. The Welsh now had no princes of their own. So, the King gave them a new, English prince – his baby son, Prince Edward. Edward was the heir to the kingdom of England. Ever since then, the eldest son and heir of the reigning King or Queen of England has had the title *Prince of Wales.*

Left: *The Princess of Wales at Caernarfon Castle.*

The Prince and Princess of Wales have been on many overseas tours since they were married. They planned to go to Australia and New Zealand in 1982, but this was put off until 1983 because the Princess was expecting her first baby, Prince William.

The Australians and New Zealanders thought it worth waiting for because the Prince and Princess brought Prince William with them.

The visit was a great success and so was the next tour, to Canada, even though William was not there this time. Everywhere the Prince and Princess went, huge crowds waited to cheer them. Everyone was very excited. They loved having the Prince and Princess in their country. Lots of people gave them presents for their little boy. As a result, William received hundreds of teddy bears!

Charles and Diana saw many interesting things, such as the famous 'Ayers Rock' in Australia. The Maoris in New Zealand took them on a trip in a 100-foot long war canoe. In Canada, Charles and Diana met Red Indians in feathered head-dresses.

Left: *The Prince and Princess of Wales at the Rotary Memorial Park, Dalhousie, Canada.*

People in Europe are also very interested in the Prince and Princess of Wales. When Charles and Diana went to Italy in 1985, they were again greeted by enormous crowds. Like the people who saw them on other overseas tours, the Italians thought Diana was very beautiful and charming. The Prince and Princess went to the Vatican, in Rome, to meet Pope John Paul II and visited famous Italian cities like Florence and Venice.

Above: *Charles and Diana enjoy a canoe ride with Maori warriors in New Zealand.*

Above: *The Prince and Princess visit the Vatican and have an audience with Pope John Paul II.*
Top right: *The Princess of Wales in Sydney during the Australian tour.*

Every year, in June, the Royal Family goes to Ascot in Berkshire to watch the horse-racing on the famous racecourse there. It is a very colourful event. The ladies wear beautiful dresses and hats. The men are dressed in long-tailed coats and top hats. The Princess of Wales is not quite as fond of horses as other members of the Royal Family but, of course, she goes to Ascot with the Queen, the Queen Mother and other 'royals'.

At Ascot, the Royal Family ride in carriages called landaus along the course where the horses will later race. They wave to the crowds of people who, of course, wave back in greeting. The Princess of Wales first rode in one of the royal carriages in 1981, two months before her wedding. The Royal Family have their own 'royal enclosure', a separate part of the grounds around the racecourse. Here, they entertain their guests and friends.

'Royal Ascot' as this meeting is known, is a great fashion event. It lasts for a whole week, so the royal ladies are seen in several different outfits and different hats to go with them. Because of the summery weather, the Princess of Wales can wear her favourite colours, and her favourite material, which is silk.

The Princess has become a sort of 'Queen of Fashion'. So everyone is interested in what she wears. Some will copy her dresses and hats and later on, they will dress just like her.

Opposite: *The Princess strolls in the Royal Enclosure at Ascot with Prince Andrew.*

Above: *The Princess rides in an open carriage with the Queen Mother at Ascot wearing a fashionable outfit in black and white.*

Before she goes out on public engagements, the Princess of Wales has to do her 'homework'. For example, in February 1985, she went to an Asian Feast at the Royal Embassy of Nepal in London. So, she had to learn in advance about Asian food, how it was cooked and how it is eaten. This knowledge is important because, like other members of the Royal Family, the Princess always speaks first when she is introduced to someone. She must know the right things to say in order to start a short conversation. The people she meets are, of course, very pleased that she has taken the trouble to learn something about them.

Diana is very good at doing her homework. Nurses she has spoken to in hospitals have praised her knowledge of medical subjects. Factory workers too, find the Princess can talk easily about industries and machinery.

Sometimes, Diana has to say something in other languages. She has made a short speech in Welsh and when she was in Italy in April 1985, she spoke some Italian. Before she did so, she practised hard and both the Welsh and Italians were delighted to hear her speak their languages.

The Princess of Wales often meets kings, queens and princesses from other countries.

Above: *The Princess of Wales visits the Cancer Centre in Kensington. She is Patron of the Malcolm Sargent Cancer Fund for children.*

She also meets foreign presidents who come to Britain on 'State Visits' as guests of the Queen. Her homework for these important occasions includes information about the visitors' countries and about the visitors themselves.

So you can see that before her engagements, the Princess must do some hard work and learn quite a lot.

***Above:** The Princess visits the Royal Blind School at Leatherhead and, as usual, is attentive to the children.*

***Right:** The Princess who is Patron of the Red Cross Society's Youth and Juniors, attends a church service in Bristol Cathedral wearing her Red Cross uniform for the first time.*

A Fashion Show Evening

Tonight, the Princess of Wales is going to a big fashion show at Grosvenor House Hotel in London. Here, she is going to see dresses designed by Bruce Oldfield. Bruce Oldfield grew up in Dr. Barnardo's, the famous children's orphanage. The Princess is President of Dr. Barnardo's and all the money raised by the fashion show will go to the orphanage.

Many of the ladies at the fashion show, including the Princess, are wearing dresses designed by Bruce Oldfield. Diana is wearing a magnificent silver dress.

Below: *Top fashion designer Bruce Oldfield, was delighted that the Princess could attend his 10th Anniversary Fashion Show, in aid of Dr. Barnado's.*

Diana's Dresses

Diana has some very beautiful dresses to wear in the evenings. The silver dress by Bruce Oldfield which she wore to the Oldfield fashion show in March 1985 was only one of them. Because the show was not a formal royal occasion, Diana could pick what she liked from her wardrobe. So, she chose something that showed off her slim figure. It was a rather unusual dress.

On other occasions, Diana wears evening dresses with very full skirts, pretty sleeves and a lot of lacy decorations on them. These dresses are usually for formal occasions, because they are the sort of dress royal ladies wear when they perform royal duties in the evening. One of these duties is attending State Banquets given at Buckingham Palace for visiting Heads of State. You can easily tell the difference between a 'formal' and an 'informal' or ordinary evening engagement. For a 'formal' engagement, the Princess of Wales and other royal ladies wear tiaras: a half-coronet worn like a head -band. Often, tiaras are made of diamonds.

Above: *Diana leaving the Bruce Oldfield Fashion Show, wearing a dress specially designed for her by Bruce Oldfield.*

The Princess arrives at half past eight and is introduced to many famous people. One of them is the television actress, Joan Collins. The Princess chats with them for a while. Then, they all go into the big ballroom where the show will take place. There are 1,000 guests. Each one paid £100 for their seat and supper with champagne. The guests sit at tables decorated with six dozen white tulips. Ringo Starr, the ex-Beatle, is there. So is Christopher Reeve, who plays Superman in films.

Left: *The Princess wears the Spencer 'Family' tiara and on her dress the Queen's Family Order.*

Opposite: *The Princess meets Dire Staits, one of her favourite pop groups, who were performing at a concert in aid of the Prince of Wales Trust.*

Diana's Jewellery

When Diana puts on her tiara for important royal occasions, she sometimes chooses the tiara which once belonged to Queen Mary: Queen Mary, who died in 1953, was the great-grandmother of Prince Charles. At other times, Diana wears the Spencer tiara, which comes from her own family. She wore this on her wedding day, to hold her white veil.

When she became engaged to Prince Charles in 1981, he gave her a beautiful engagement ring with a sapphire surrounded by diamonds. At about this time, she was also seen wearing a diamond watch. After the birth of Prince William in 1982, Charles gave his wife a gorgeous diamond necklace: it was decorated with a heart-shaped diamond. Diana also has a gold necklace given to her by her husband. It has a round medallion with one word — 'William' — written on it in Charles' handwriting.

The Princess sits at a table opposite the stage where the fashion models will show the dresses. There are about twelve models who will show more than one hundred day and evening dresses. The fashion show, which lasts for half an hour, ends with a model coming on to the stage wearing a beautiful wedding gown.

After supper, Kid Creole and the Coconuts play music for dancing. The Princess of Wales dances with several guests. Everyone can see that she has thoroughly enjoyed herself. But then, the time comes to go home and the Princess leaves the hotel just before midnight.

Above: *Superstars meet Royal Superstars. Diana and Charles meet the champion Olympic skaters, Torvill and Dean at a gala Ice Show in aid of Help the Hospices.*

Evenings Out

The most exciting engagements for the Prince and Princess of Wales often take place in the evenings. This is when they attend events like the ice show by Torvill and Dean, the famous Olympic skaters, or the first showings of big films like 'Amadeus' or 'A View to A Kill', the new James Bond picture. They also go to concerts given by famous singing stars like Neil Diamond or groups like Duran Duran, Genesis and Dire Straits. The Princess is an enthusiastic pop music fan, so she enjoys these concerts very much, especially as they help to raise money for charity. For example, the world-wide Live Aid Rock Concert the Prince and Princess attended on 13th July 1985 helped to raise £50 millions to help poor and hungry people in Ethiopia.

When the Prince and Princess support charities by coming to fund-raising concerts, people can see these charities are important. So, they give their support too.

Opposite: *The Princess arrives at the Royal Premier of Amadeus in aid of the Royal College of Music's Centenary Appeal.*

Below: *Prince Charles and the Princess had a wonderful time at the Live Aid concert organised by pop star Bob Geldof.*

The Princess Helping People

The Royal Family is interested in the well-being of ordinary people. So, they become Presidents or Patrons of organisations which work to help, or improve the lives of the people. This interest is of great benefit. The Royal Family are very, very important people. So, they can easily persuade others to give *their* help and support.

As you know, the Princess of Wales is especially concerned about children. On her public engagements, children can always be sure of a special smile from her. The Princess was very happy to become President of Dr. Barnardo's Homes for Children or Patron of the Pre-School Playgroups Association which deals with very young children under the age of five.

The Princess is also interested in helping disabled people and agreed to become patron of two organisations for the blind and two for the deaf. In all, she has eighteen patronages. These include music organisations and several organisations in the Principality of Wales. She is also Patron of Help the Aged.

Above: *The Royal Air Force flies the Princess to Liverpool to visit a Dr. Barnado's home.*

Above: *The Princess, who is the President of the National Deaf, Blind and Rubella Association visits a school in Ealing.*

Right: *The Princess is Patron of the London City Ballet and flew to Oslo to attend a performance of Carmen by the Company.*

The Princess goes to the Ballet

Diana loves ballet. When she was a child, she wanted to become a ballet dancer, but she grew to be too tall. So, she was specially delighted when she was asked to become Patron of the London City Ballet in July 1983. The Princess is so keen about the Ballet that she watches the dancers rehearsing (practising). In February 1984, she travelled all the way to Oslo, in Norway, to see the first performance of their new ballet, 'Carmen'.

Diana's Holidays

The Princess of Wales, like the rest of the Royal Family, works hard during most of the year. She really deserves her holidays, and also the relaxing weekends she spends with her husband and children at their country home, Highgrove House. When she has a 'day off' in London, the Princess likes to 'go shopping in secret' — this means visiting the shops like any ordinary person and walking round the counters of big department stores. Very often though, people recognise her and her shopping isn't secret any more!

Because she is so famous, the Princess finds it difficult to have the privacy (being alone) she needs to enjoy her holidays. Privacy is fairly easy to find at Balmoral Castle in Scotland, where the Princess spends part of the summer with her family and her royal relatives, or at Windsor Castle, where the Royal Family get together at Christmas. But in Liechtenstein, where the Prince and Princess go skiing in the winter, they must let newspaper photographers take their pictures before they are left alone to enjoy their holiday.

Charles and Diana also like the sunshine and have had holidays on Eleuthera, one of the beautiful, warm Bahama islands in the Caribbean. For Diana, holidays mean she can do some of the things she has little time for during the rest of the year. She likes watching television, seeing films, listening to pop records, reading romantic novels, photography and watching her husband play polo.

Left: *Charles and Diana like to relax from their busy schedule on a skiing holiday.*

Above: *Although the weather was unkind, Diana and Charles enjoyed visiting the Western Isles. The 'Royals' have spent many happy holidays in Scotland.*

Left: *Prince Charles, a champion polo player, happily receiving the winner's cup from his wife at Windsor.*

Diana's Birthdays

The Princess of Wales was born on 1st July 1961. She became engaged to Prince Charles just over four months before her twentieth birthday in 1981. That was an exciting birthday, for she was preparing for her wedding, which took place four weeks later, on 29th July, 1981.

Since she became a member of the Royal Family, Diana has spent other birthdays quietly at home with her family. But there was one that was very different and very exciting: her twenty-second birthday on 1st July, 1983.

That day, the Prince and Princess of Wales were almost at the end of their visit to Canada. Diana received lots of birthday cards and dozens of flowers. There was a message from her mother-in-law, the Queen, in London, and another from her father-in-law, Prince Philip, who was also in Canada at the time. Prince Charles gave Diana a present of jewellery, and when they arrived for the opening ceremony of the World University Games in Edmonton, Alberta, thousands of people were waiting to sing *Happy Birthday to You* for the Princess.

Later the same day, the Prince and Princess boarded the aircraft that would take them home to England. During the flight, there was a champagne birthday party. Diana received two birthday cakes. One was from the crew of the aircraft and it said: *Love from Canada,* in icing. The other was from Prince Charles, and the icing said: *I Love You, Darling.*

DIANA — a truly 'Royal' Princess.

Acknowledgements
Written by: Brenda Ralph-Lewis
Brenda Ralph-Lewis is a prolific writer of 'Royal' books. She has worked for many years on studies of The Royal Family and has gained a marvellous insight into their very busy lives.

Photographs supplied by kind permission of:
Rex Features: All photographs except:
Tim Graham: Page 5 – lower, 15 – lower right, 16 – left, 19, 24 – both, 29, 38, 45 – above, 47.
Alistair McDavid: Page 40.

Published by Studio Publications (Ipswich) Limited
32 Princes Street, Ipswich IP1 1RJ England

Printed and bound in Great Britain

Paperback ISBN 0 86215 324 7
Hardback ISBN 0 86215 314 X